Energy Makes Things Work

We all need electricity.

Electricity is **energy.**

Electricity is the energy that makes things work.

Look at the television.

Electricity will make it work.

Look at the refrigerator.

Electricity will make it work.

Here is my scooter.

Look at the wheels.

The wheels will go **round**.

11

Electricity will make the wheels go round ...
and round ...

... and round.

Glossary

energy

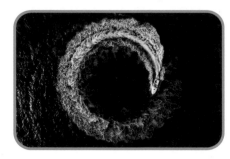

round

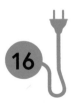